TALES FR(
PINFOLD FARM
Growing up in Yardley
in the early 1900s

HELEN PITT

The Birmingham Local History Series Volume 1

APS BOOKS
Stourbridge

Tales From Pinfold Farm
Copyright ©2018 APS Publications

Front cover from the work of the early Sutton Coldfield photographer William Morris Grundy
Back cover extract from 1888 Ordnance Survey

ISBN 9781912309641

APS Publications,
4 Oakleigh Road,
Stourbridge,
West Midlands,
DY8 2JX

www.andrewsparke.com

This book is dedicated to the memory of my darling mum Bess, who penned most of these enchanting tales and to all of my cousins, especially Jean, Anne, John and Paul, because the old farm still means a lot to us all.

Bess Pitt nee Mansfield-Huntley
3/7/1911 - 3/3/1995

Introduction
Pinfold Farm, Yardley 1911

My mother Bess, christened Lillian Mansfield-Huntley, loved to write. When she was in her fifties she decided to put pen to paper about her recollections of growing up on Pinfold Farm, situated in Mansfield Road in Yardley, five miles east of Birmingham city centre. Mum was born on July 3rd 1911 and died peacefully in her sleep eighty-two years later. Occasionally pieces of her writing would be published in Birmingham Evening Mail, an achievement she was terribly proud of and she would sometimes be invited to be a guest speaker by local history societies. My mother was a warm, witty and confident, irreverent (some would say bawdy), woman and lots of people enjoyed her writing and anecdotes some of which I have reproduced in these pages.

After my mother died in 1995, many of her bits and pieces were lost or sold and so it was with huge delight that I rediscovered some of her recollections sixteen years after she died. It is thanks to my wonderful cousins, sisters Jean and Anne (nee Huntley) who passed her notes to me to record here, that some of those memories have endured.

All this is therefore really the work of my mother, Bess except for the last chapter which was written by my cousin Anne.

Tales from Pinfold Farm

The back garden at Pinfold Farm.

1
The Farm

My brother's name is Seba but we all called him Sid. My name is Lillian, and everyone calls me Bess. Here are some details of our life as children at Pinfold Farm in the early nineteen-hundreds.

Sid was christened Seba Mansfield-Huntley after Seba, a great grandson of Noah and brother of the mighty warrior, Nimrod. This name was a traditional one in the Mansfield family. Mansfield is the family name of our mother who also had a brother called Seba. The brother, our Uncle Seba, met an unusual end. He was haymaking in the fields when he was stung on the tongue by a bee or a wasp. His tongue swelled up like a balloon and choked poor Uncle Seba to death.

We were born at Pinfold Farm in South Yardley, at a time when the building still functioned as a farm with cows and smells and things. We lived there with our parents and our sister Muriel for some years. Muriel had cerebral palsy and we looked after her as she grew up and stopped boys from bullying her, calling her names and throwing stones. The farm was originally called Penfold Farm because there used to be a pound or pen there, where stray animals were kept until collected by their owners. From trade directories, there have been Mansfields farming in Yardley from at least 1820, when a William and Mary were listed as farmers. It is not until 1875 that we find a Mrs. Mary Anne Mansfield farming at Pinfold Farm. She could possibly be our grandmother or perhaps our Aunty Annie.

Note: The farm is still there on the corner of Mansfield Road. It was in a state of dereliction but is now restored as a family home. It is a Grade Two listed building.

The farm is now rather grandly called Pinfold House, but it has lost most of its land, only retaining a small back garden that drops away to a no man's land leading down to the Grand Union Canal which runs through Yardley. The no man's land used to be a sand pit, serving the local community and I remember local people collecting sand by the barrow load. The pit was controlled by the residents of a house beside the old canal bridge.

Next to Pinfold House there was a complex of redundant garages and such like where the farm sheds used to be. Sid referred to them as the rick-yard, fold-yard and milking shed but there may have been other yards and barns. There was certainly a fully equipped blacksmith's shop, but no blacksmith. The fold-yard was also used to pen stray animals until their owners could collect them upon payment of a small fee. One item of farm machinery that Sid remembers is a horse 'whim' in the fold yard where the poor horse would walk round and around in circles driving a chaff cutting machine. On windy days there was a good deal of dust generated by this machine. There was also a deposit of grain of course which attracted the sparrows.

One day as Sid recalls, he became aware of a rat using the pond in the yard. There were several pipes that led into the pond and Sid was unsure which one the rat was using. Sid kept watch, sitting in a shed with his catapult at the ready, waiting for the appearance of the rat. Our mother became aware of his absence and came to find him. When Sid had explained what it was that he was doing, she suggested that he would do much better using his father's walking stick gun. He knew where the gun was, and mother supplied the cartridges. Sid sat down again in the shed and waited perhaps for an hour when suddenly, the rat appeared. Sid took careful aim, raising the gun to his eye and peering down the barrel, but the gun had no shoulder stock. When Sid fired the gun, it jumped back in his hands and bounced off his face. Sid never knew whether he hit the rat, but his face and eye turned black and blue, giving him the unenviable task of explaining his injuries to our father.

Note: Their father was a disciplinarian. Sid and Bess knew whenever Sid was in trouble, because father would stand at the gate to the farm and unbuckle his belt, ready to thrash Sid when he was returning home.

2
The Kitchen

A picture of the kitchen gradually emerges from Sid's memories and Bess's notes certainly confirm the picture. The stone flagged kitchen seems to have been the most occupied room in the farm. The wall that looked out over the fold-yard had small arched windows with bars and by one of these was a small table. Along another wall was a wooden settle and I imagine that in the centre of the room a large table would have stood that was used for preparing meals and devouring them on less formal occasions.

The dominant feature of the room was the large open fire. It was alight almost continuously and at times was used to cook the family meals. In Sid's recollection, it was fired by buckets of coke, sometimes two or three at a time. Across the hearth stretched a long spit, suspended by two black iron 'dogs', which rotated the meat very slowly. Beneath the meat there stood a very large pan to catch the meat juices as they fell. The juice was used by whoever was passing by to baste the meat to ease the burning. Gravy was also prepared on the fire. Sid remembers his Aunty May (Wakefield) crouching there with a ladle or spoon full of sugar held over the fire. When it turned brown it was used as the gravy browning. For other cooking there was a coal or coke fired double oven that had large, flat plates to heat the black iron cooking pots. On one of the walls was Sid's father's muzzle loading duck gun and some gunpowder flasks.

Sid's great uncle Will, who was probably his mother's uncle, sat in the kitchen at times with a loaded gun and shot the sparrows who searched the chaff in the fold yard for grain. The wretched corpses were then gathered up and made into Uncle Will's favourite delicacy, sparrow pie. Uncle Will also had a very proud boast; he had never done a day's work in his life. He often stood outside the farm, leaning on the fence by the brewhouse with his big belly protruding and exchanging the time of day with passers-by.

"How be master, Willum?" came the query.

"I moan't grumble," would be the reply.

At other times Will could be found within the house, often with his gramophone complete with its brassy trumpet, playing his favourite tune. This was a recording of the famous Harry Lauder singing 'Keep Right on to the End of the Road.' It seemed to be played repeatedly with Uncle Will accompanying the chorus. Bess recalls him as being rather eccentric. He didn't believe the world was round. Nor could he understand the presence of aeroplanes. But there are other stories about Uncle Will or *The Guv'nor* as he became known and the following anecdote is verbatim from Bess's notes.

One day Will was taking a ride on the shaft of a hay wagon when he slipped off. The iron rim of the rear wheel rolled over his right wrist. He rose to his feet, got back on the shaft and brought the horses and the wagon safely back into the rick-yard. He walked over to the pump and pumped ice cold well water over his crushed wrist until it went numb. He then went into the kitchen where his sister, Ann Maria sat by the open fire in her black leather chair.

He told her what had happened to him and he instructed her to bring a cloth and some scissors. She cut the linen cloth into strips and tightly bound his wrist. He took a long swig of whiskey from a pewter jug which was always kept in the kitchen cupboard. He then lay down on the black, horsehair sofa under the wall clock. He remained there for best part of a week, only getting up from beneath the check horse blanket when he needed the lavatory - a good-ish step to the end of the garden! At the end of the week he gradually resumed his various tasks around the farm and in due course, made a complete recovery using his wrist much as before. He sometimes complained of *the rheumatics*, but at no time did it occur to him to trouble the doctor.

3
The Guv'nor

When *the Guv'nor* was in his sixties, he developed a lump in his groin which of course he never mentioned. One day, Sid's mother found him doubled up in pain on the wooden settle in the kitchen, his head on the table, groaning loudly. She was terrified enough to send for *the chap*, as they referred to a friend called Frank Bradley, to go and fetch the doctor. The doctor was a dapper little Welshman called Price who often called in at the farm on his morning rounds. His visits were purely social as he was well acquainted with the pewter jug in the kitchen cupboard. On these visits he would stand with his back to the fire, a glass in his hand and try and convince Willum that the world was indeed round and not flat as Willum firmly believed.

On this visit however, he quickly diagnosed a strangulated hernia which required urgent attention. The family were united in refusing to allow the Guv'nor to go to hospital as people died there, so it was decided that the urgent operation must be carried out at the farm. The front parlour was rapidly prepared; furniture was carried out and clean sheets were spread about. The large kitchen table was carried into the room and scrubbed until it was spotless. All the spare oil lamps were assembled in the room as there was no electricity in the house. Every utensil was filled with water to be boiled on the kitchen range. The Guv'nor undressed and put on his nightshirt and in due course, an eminent specialist arrived along with his registrar, two nurses and an anaesthetist. This major operation was then carried out on the kitchen table with absolute success. The Guv'nor made a complete recovery and lived on for many more years.

Another eccentric member of the family who Bess recalled was second cousin Lily who was a dress maker by profession. She was of medium height with black, frizzy hair which she washed with a paraffin rinse because she firmly believed that this action would stop her hair from turning grey. As she was rather fat and perspired freely, she did not smell as sweetly as her name implied. Lily favoured floral material for her dresses which usually had four pointed cuffs, sashes and lots of frills. Her face was pale and full, like the moon and she had a large brown mole on the side of her nose. She had lost a tooth here and there, but she was an incurable romantic and never lost hope that one day, a handsome young farmer would come along and sweep her off her feet. Sadly, he never did.

To watch the daily ritual that Lily undertook in preparation for a meal was a feast by itself. She would lift a seat cushion and then take two elastic bands and a copy of the evening newspaper. She draped the points of her sleeves over each wrist and put a band on each one. This was to prevent the cuffs from trailing in the gravy. She then took a folded sheet of newspaper and cut a large, U-shaped piece out of it. This was then opened and placed over her head and round her neck like a huge bib. The object of this was to catch any bits of food that fell from her fork because she shovelled her food into her mouth with amazing speed.

On summer Sunday evenings when the family were all assembled, Lily, wearing one of her latest creations, would go into the garden and pick as large a flower as she could find, usually a full-blown rose or a deep red peony. The flower would then be pinned to her ample bosom. She played the zither quite well and sang in a high, sweet voice. The family were then treated to a recital of ballads such as 'Pale Hands I Loved Beside the Shalimar,' 'The Sheik of Araby,' or maybe, 'Where My Caravan Has Rested.' The songs were accompanied with many elaborate hand movements as she played the little harp.

4
Great Aunt Lizzie

Lily had a younger sister May who was a much smaller version of Lily except that May was not in the least romantic. In fact she was rather dour and spoke but little. She was however, always kind to Bess and sometimes in the afternoon they would both go into May's small bedroom up in the roof, with its sloping ceiling. Under the window May kept a large trunk. It mostly contained clothes but deep within was May's pride and joy. She kept it wrapped in a shawl and it was a beautiful doll that she called Jane. It had a wax face with blue, staring eyes and her body was made of kid. She wore a blue dress with a pinafore, a white bonnet with pink flowers and little white kid shoes. May would allow Bess to sit on her bed and nurse Jane while May changed her clothes and combed her hair. What happened to the doll in the end is not known but she was dearly loved.

The mother of Lily and May was Great Aunt Lizzie. She was a truly terrifying old lady, tall and upright with white hair and a deep voice. She always wore ankle length dresses with high necks and sometimes she had a jet brooch at her throat. She frequently quoted the bible and often exhorted the children to 'turn the other cheek' or employed other biblical aphorisms. One day Great Aunt Lizzie discovered one of the hens eating its own eggs in the hen run. Her reaction was immediate. She fetched a chopper from the woodshed and while she held the unfortunate bird down with her foot, chopped off its head. The body of the chicken got up and ran for yards before dropping to the ground, twitching. The sight produced nightmares in the children for weeks.

Great Aunt Lizzie had a long-standing feud with her sister Ann Maria. They didn't speak to each other for twenty years and not even on Lizzie's death bed did a word pass. Forgiveness was not in their nature!

Apart from the horses and the horse drawn carriages, Sid and Bess's experience of travel was limited. It was thus greeted with great delight when a farming friend of the family, Ted Lee, visited them. Ted had farmed Dovehouse Farm in Solihull and had just sold it saying that he'd had no idea just how much he was worth. With some of the proceeds of the sale Ted bought a brand-new Model T Ford. It was a great honour and a privilege for Sid and Bess to be allowed to sit in it and be ogled enviously by passers-by. The family had once been taken by Uncle Ted, as the children referred to him, to Dovehouse Farm for dinner and the children were most excited with the joys of car travel. Uncle Ted even asked them if they were going fast enough, they were doing thirty miles an hour but to Sid and Bess, it seemed if as they were flying.

Sid related a story about an employee of Ted Lee. The man was a long serving farm labourer who lived happily with his wife in a tied cottage at Dovehouse Farm. One day the 'phone rang and the call was for this labourer also called Ted. Now remember, the telephone was a new- fangled invention and very few people had the privilege of owning one. This being so, the labourer had never spoken to the 'phone and refused to come and talk to the instrument. The matter was urgent and so the police were contacted and asked to take the news to the farm hand. It was to tell him that his brother had died and left him his farm in Wiltshire and all his money. The labourer refused his inheritance saying, "I don't want no dyud man's money. Me and the wife are happy here and we don't want no dyud man's money..."

5
Transport

The pleasure of sitting in Ted Lee's car must have awoken a yearning in Sid because while he was still in his youth he bought a belt-driven Triumph motor cycle on which he patrolled the neighbourhood. He went further afield on it of course, driving to Lapworth to go fishing and to Chessett's Wood where an aunt lived. The aunt was probably on his father's side of the family because on one memorable occasion, Sid's father rode pillion with him on a trip down there. After driving through Knowle, Sid encountered a very sharp left- hand bend which he and his pillion passenger had to negotiate the bike around. Sid of course leaned into the corner, but his father didn't. Happily, for them both, the corner was negotiated but only because both sides of the road were used! A lecture on how to ride pillion on a motorbike was then administered to Sid's father before the journey was continued. His father liked the motorcycle but never learned how to control it properly. He tried riding it round the fold-yard but with too many revs and a great deal of on/off clutch action. It was a good job the machine was belt-driven.

Sid replaced the motor cycle with a Clyno car, a two-seater with a dicky seat in the rear. This car became Sid's pride and joy and he enjoyed taking various friends and relatives for rides in it. For his Uncle Will, it was his first time in a motor car and he wasn't terribly impressed with the seats. They were far too low! Uncle Will went into the brew house and rummaged around until he emerged with a beer crate. This he placed on the passenger seat and perched himself upon the crate. Now he was at the *proper* height - for a pony and trap at least. He then allowed Sid to drive him around the local lanes. Uncle Will could see quite clearly over the hedge rows, but Sid recalls that he blushed quite red with the embarrassment.

6
The Brew House.

Further along Mansfield Road there is an off-license with a house attached. This had been given to Bess and Sid's mother as a twenty-first birthday present. The family were evidently well off in those days. It was kept by their mother as a beer off-license. She didn't live in the house part of the premises although they were furnished. Sid recalled that the new off-license replaced his mother's earlier brewing enterprise where the beer was sold from the farm itself. She had brewed her own beer in premises close to the farm at the rear of the fold yard. There could be found two large vats and behind these, the boiler house. The produce of all this industry was a beer called Mansfield Beer which was sold fresh from the barrel. She also sold stout, but this was delivered in barrels to the farm and was bottled there with Sid and Bess sticking the labels onto the bottles.

The off-license was a popular place, with people coming for their beer from up to a mile away and before opening time, a queue had often developed. There would be all manner of working men or their sons standing in line, clutching their jugs or bottles ready to receive the beer. Some of the sons who had been sent on the errand by their fathers, would swig the cold beer down their throats without pause. Then it was back to the queue again to get their jugs topped up. Angry fathers would come to the farm, thinking they had been *diddled*, so from then on, the beer was sold only in bottles and paper caps were sealed on to the top of them, so the sons could not drink their father's beer on the way home.

To help around the farm and to do the brewing, the family employed a man from Kidderminster called Frank Bradley. Frank was a red-faced, bull-necked man with an accent so thick you needed a translator to understand him. Still, he did the milking and must have made a good job of the brewing. Like many a farm labourer in those days, Frank slept in and ate with the family except that he had his own table, under the window where Uncle Will shot sparrows. At this table Frank sat, reading his comics which he thoroughly enjoyed, bursting into gales of laughter at the choicest pieces. He slept in his own room which was small and situated over the brewhouse. During the day he had found his own room in the barns near the fold yard and this was called *Frank's Hut.*

He was a 'queer fellow', recalls Sid and cited two examples of his oddness. To move the heavier items around the farm there was a four-wheeled truck, rather like a railway porter's trolley. One day, Bess was playing on this trolley in the fold yard when it rolled away with her and dumped her into a vat of water. Frank burst into laughter and was so helpless with mirth, he was quite unable to pull her out, so someone else was called for the task. On another emergency Frank was again unable to assist, when the farm collie took hold of Bess's arm and wouldn't let go.

Bess and Sid (Seba) circa 1928

Frank was regarded as quite old and so he surprised them all when he left the farm to get married. That heralded the end of the home-made beer business and from that point onwards, the beer was bought in.

Note from the author: In 1983, I lived in a house on the Yardley Road which was being renovated. Beneath the floorboards at the front of the house we found an ancient bottle of Mansfield Beer which somebody, (I like to think it was Sid,) had placed there for posterity. A little message from the past, from my grandma to me.

7
The Ghost

Bess and Sid often spoke of Pinfold farm being haunted. Bess recorded that the apparition of an elderly lady, clothed in a grey dress down to her ankles, her white hair gathered into a bun, appeared to many people at various times at the top of the staircase at Pinfold Farm.

Sid spoke of one spooky event that occurred when their father was at the end of his life. Bess had contacted him to say that if he wanted to see his father while he was still alive, then he should hurry to his bedside. Sid did rush but sadly, he was too late. He was standing there beside his father's bed, head bent quietly in sorrow when he heard a mighty rushing and rustling noise on the stairs, a noise which roused him from his grief. Sid turned and opened the door to the stairs to discover that all the wallpaper had fallen off the walls. This might well be coincidence but Sid couldn't stop wondering what made it fall off at that precise moment?

On another occasion guests were being entertained at the farm overnight. The farmhouse was large and had a long landing at the top of the stairs which led to all the bedrooms. Two couples were accommodated either side of the stairs. That night, after all in the house had retired to bed and were sound asleep, the visitors were awoken by loud bumps and bangs on the landing. They rushed to fling open their bedroom doors only to find themselves gazing at each other. There was nothing visible to cause the noises which had by then in any case ceased. Sid's two sisters Bess and Muriel shared a bedroom and often spoke of 'bumps in the night'.

During the family's ownership of the farm, Sid and Bess's father had cause to rent it to a family and the Mansfields moved out to live at 263 Yardley Road. The new tenants also experienced the ghost when one dark evening the old man of the family was making his nightly trek to the outside loo. He was suddenly stopped in his tracks when he saw a lady in a crinoline dress on the path before him. His errand forgotten, he hastily returned to the house in a very frightened state to relate what he had seen. Needless to say; the lady had gone when the others went to investigate the old man's sighting.

Note: The outside loo features in two episodes of these tales and from my mother Bess's recollections it seems to have been a deluxe throne room. It was in the garden, no water to flush it of course but it did have three holes carved out of the wooden seat, large, medium and small.

More humorous recollections concern Sid and Bess's Aunty Annie. She must have been a prim, Victorian lady and was usually dressed in a crinoline frock with a white apron in front. She used to sit with her money on her lap counting the value of it and when folk passed her by, she would cover her money with the hem of her apron. It was the same aunty Annie who was treading warily to the outside closet one night guided by the glimmer of her candle. The glimmer also attracted a marauding owl who swooped down to the candle and onto Aunty Annie. There is no record of what happened to the candle or to the owl for the startled aunt fled in a panic from the scene.

Aunty Annie seems to have been the moneyed member of the family for she had built two shops and a house in Yardley Road and also possibly financed the building of houses in Tiffield Road. She herself lived in one of the shops or at 263. Sid and Bess often had meals or slept there as children for their mother and father worked long hours at the off license.

In the back garden at Aunty Annie's house was a large and very old apple tree from which she insisted on having the first fruit as her right. On the morning of her death, the apple tree died also and was found fallen across the garden, its leaves scattering in the breeze.

8
A Busy Father

Unusually, Bess and Sid's father didn't farm. This was left to their Uncle Tom with Frank Bradley's assistance and to these two men fell the tasks around the farm. Most of these were associated with pastoral farming, with half a dozen cows, two horses, hens and chickens. The hardest labour would have been haymaking in the rick-yard. Though Sid and Bess's dad wasn't the farmer of the household, nevertheless he regaled the children with tales of a deaf and dumb cockerel and a one-eyed chicken. The poor chicken eventually died from starvation because his beak never went to where his eye told him the food was! No, their father wasn't a farmer, but he did work hard.

His day job, in modern parlance, was as a clerk for the railways at Curzon Street in Birmingham city centre. He set off early in the morning and returned late in the evening for they worked long hours in those days, even in offices. He partook of his evening meal wherever Sid and Bess happened to be and then it was back to work again at the off-license where he would assist the children's mother. This activity finished at eleven o'clock and then it was straight to bed.

At the weekend father would harness up the four-wheeled dray and set off on his beer delivery round in Acocks Green, returning with the empties. On some occasions he took the dray further afield to Saltley to collect coke for the fires in the house and the brewery boiler room. There was also a regular trip to Ansell's Brewery in Aston to collect spent hops. These would be mixed with chaff and so on to be fed to the cows in winter. Despite all this activity, the family became poorer because Sid and Bess's father had two weaknesses, horses and drink. This is not to say that these were excessive, more that they presented a constant drain on the family purse.

The job at the railway conferred travel privileges on Sid and Bess's family; they could travel cheaply along the London, Midland and Scottish Railway routes as far as the sea crossing to Ireland if they felt the urge. Despite this, my grandmother made no use of this facility and the furthest she ever travelled on the train was to the Bull Ring in Birmingham city centre.

Across Yardley Road from the farm were some other barns which did not belong to Pinfold. It was here that a man called George Leech pursued his living. George was a *Jack of all country trades* spending much time as a horse dealer and also working as a milkman. He wended his way to his customers driving a pony and trap with the churns on the back. Customers came to Mr. Leech with their jugs to be filled from the measure on his churn. He usually wore a brimmed hat and on rainy days, the water would collect in his brim and could be seen to be added to the churn by accident, as he bent over to fill his measure. He was not the only milkman to ply his wares in the area because there was also an old man on a bicycle who sold milk although how much milk he could carry on the back of the bicycle is questionable.

Aunt Lillian, cousin Jean and grandad George in the parlour at Pinfold.c1958

To return to George Leech, Sid recalled that once, George bought a pony for his daughter at Henley-in-Arden Horse Market. On his return home the young girl was most searching in her questions about her new pony who she hadn't yet seen, asking "What colour is he? How large is he?" and the like. When she asked about how long it's tail was her father replied, "Just long enough to cover its decency!"

9
Canal Capers

After the First World War there were three horses on the farm, Captain Tommy, Darky and Daisy. They could sometimes be found in the rick-yard and at others in Tiffield road with the cows. It was Daisy's job to take the trap out when the family went visiting. In her later years poor old Daisy became quite feeble and suffered with rheumatism. On occasions she couldn't get up off the ground after her sleep (I know the feeling well!) Captain Tommy was a good, strong horse and rather attached to Daisy, so he would help her rise by grabbing her mane or tail and pulling. Captain Tommy was an ex-army horse who had served in France pulling gun-carriages. His military upbringing showed when one of the all too frequent funerals of army personnel took place across the road at Yardley cemetery. No sooner had Captain Tommy heard the regimental band playing than he was rushing around his field, ears pricked up and prancing in recognition of past comrades.

Across the road from Tiffield is the Grand Union Canal. One afternoon when Bess's mother and father were courting, they had walked down to the tow path for a stroll when suddenly they heard a splash. Father charged down the tow path until he came upon a bald-headed man in the water. Throwing his coat off, father proceeded to rescue him with assistance from another passer-by. They got the man to the bank safely; apparently, he had been attempting suicide. On another occasion again while he was out on a stroll, he noticed a throng of spectators including a sailor in full uniform, up on the canal bridge. They were all watching a woman struggling in the water. She was up to her waist, frantically trying to save her child from the bottom of the canal. Father plunged in and rescued the child from what might otherwise have been a watery grave.

Cousin Anne's Wartime Recollections.

My Nanna shopped for her meat at Cunningtons on the Yardley Road. Tom the butcher looked after her well and she could always get plenty of black market butter. At my Nanna's house everything was washed up and put away at two in the afternoon and Nanna would go to her bed to put her curlers in and have a rest. Aunty Lil would play patience while Aunty Mu and my granddad would go to sleep. Peter the spaniel would lie on the rug by the fire and make bad smells. Muriel would fetch out the Zoflora and splash it about to hide the smell.

Nanna would get up at around four o'clock for tea with her hair all brushed and her rouge and makeup on. Wearing a smart frock with a necklace and rings on her fingers, she would make a pot of tea. This was the only menial task she would perform; she had never cooked anything in her life and wouldn't know how to. Tea would consist of very thin bread and butter spread with home-made jam or lemon curd. Sometimes there would be very thin cucumber sandwiches and always a lovely home-made cake and jam tarts.

In the evenings, the family would sit around and listen to *Dick Barton, Special Agent* on the radio. In the large garden grandpa grew lots of lovely flowers and lots of soft fruit. In the middle of the lawn he had a pear tree. Grandpa would take out his penknife from his pocket and slice up a juicy pear for my sister Barbara and me. Incidentally he also prized dandelions out of the lawn with the same penknife.

In 1939 war was declared and we had moved to Aldershaw Road, Daddy was a driver and was exempt from service. Mummy was expecting my brother John at the time and tension was very high. We lived near the Rover works at Acocks Green where munitions were being made and this building was targeted night after night by the German bombers. The sirens would sound out and we would be lifted out of our beds and taken down to the bottom of the garden to take cover in a cold, damp air-raid shelter which was constructed from sheets of corrugated iron and covered with earth. Inside were bench-like seats. Mummy would carry a box with her containing all our birth certificates for safe-keeping. When the *all clear* siren sounded, Daddy would go up to the house and make a cup of tea for us all and bring it back to the shelter. Sometimes when we went back to our beds, we would find pieces of shrapnel which had gone through the roof of our house, scattered on the beds.

One night - the night of the Coventry raids, it was particularly horrendous, and my mother was heavily pregnant. Daddy put us all in his motor and took us to Dorsington, near Stratford-upon-Avon to stay with our Aunty Ag, Uncle Jim and cousins Valerie and Richard Hodges. On the journey and just before we arrived in the pitch-black night, we drove through a flood. My mother panicked, she thought we had driven into the river and would meet a worse end than the one we had just fled from.

Our brother John was born on December 31st that year. Later, we were evacuated to my other grandfather's house at Long Marston where at five years of age, I attended the village school. At the little school all the pupils from five to fourteen were taught in one class room. There was a large, black coke stove in the room and a big girl called Megan taught me to knit. In the toilet, newspaper was cut into squares and hung on a piece of string – for loo paper.

My grandfather had a housekeeper called Suzie. She used to take the train to Stratford on a Friday to shop and would bring back fish and chips for the adults and fish cakes and chips for me and Barbara.

My grandpa Davis kept hens and grew his own vegetables. Barbara and I would go out into the hedgerows and collect pigeon eggs to make cakes as everything was rationed because of the war.

We moved back to Birmingham when John was still small. At five minutes to eight every morning the siren would blow at the Rover works and that was our cue to leave home and commence the hour long walk to school. We ate sandwiches at lunchtime with the Trenfields; there were no school dinners in those days. The Trenfields would say we were rich and they were '*poooooor*'. Nanna did not approve of the Trenfields. She was a bit of a snob and so we ended up being given a halfpenny each to cover the bus fare, so we could go home for our dinners. Grandma would serve up a whole leg of mutton for dinner on a huge meat dish. Carrots and onions would be floating in the lovely gravy. Sometimes we would have rabbit stew with triangles of crisp toast to mop up the gravy. Each day we had a huge milk pudding and a fruit pie with custard.

Aunty Lilly was a talented seamstress and would make lovely dresses for Barbara and me. We always had new clothes for Easter from Nanna and new brown sandals with white ankle socks which were the Easter tradition. I don't remember being given Easter eggs though.

During the war sugar was rationed by coupons and we would have our sweets and chocolate shared out on a Sunday. I remember walking home from school one day and offering a friend called David Gallon a sweet from my bag of goodies. I had only two squares of Cadbury's chocolate left, and he broke one off and ate it. My heart sank for that missing piece of chocolate, whereas today we have too much of everything.

Jean arrived later but that, as they say, is another story.

Scribe's note: Ann still has the box that her mother kept the birth certificates in during the war. My daughter Rebecca sometimes wears one of my grandmother's rings, a little finger ring of gold with a tiny garnet in it and when I see it, I am reminded of the grandma I never met. She died from breast cancer a few weeks before my birth, but I have in my mind's eye an image of her as clear as day, pouring out the tea at Pinfold Farm.

Epilogue

After the death of my grandparents in the early nineteen fifties, Sid and Bess decided to sell up the farm. It was a sad day losing all the paraphernalia that existed to keep the Victorian farmer at one with the world. Gone were the duck guns, walking stick gun and their powder flasks. The four-poster bed went, the table and chairs too. A heavy wooden sideboard was also sold and when it was manhandled away from the wall where it had stood for a century, beneath it, written on the stone floor backwards in chalk was the word, 'wait'.

Sid and Bess wondered if it was a message from the resident ghost, trying to tell them something. Bess wiped the chalk away but the following day the word had returned so that's where it stayed. The sisters and Sid moved out and the farm was purchased by a man from along the road, Mr. Leonard, for around £2,000. He was most proud of the ghost and a write up appeared in a Sunday newspaper with a picture of an old lady in a crinoline dress. It was not the ghost of course but a photograph of dear old Aunty Annie.

Sid stayed at 263 Yardley Road where he plied the trade of a florist quite successfully until he moved to pastures new in Throckmorton.

Sid and Bess's sister Muriel, who was disabled, went to live with aunt Lillian in a small cottage in Knowle. When Lillian died Muriel then went to live with Bess, my mum and Aunty Mu passed away when I was about thirteen years old.

My mother and father lived out their lives in a wonderful, rambling flat above the Midland Bank in Acocks Green.

Pinfold Farm or Pinfold House as it is now named, remained in a state of great disrepair for many years. In 2012 it was auctioned and bought for around £85,000 and sympathetically restored as a family home. The brew house was bought and converted to a home. The off-license is still there and is a local store which still sells alcohol. Pinfold House and the old brew house are Grade Two listed buildings and remain wonderful examples of Georgian period dwellings.

Pinfold Farm from Yardley Cemetery - 1958

Printed in Great Britain
by Amazon